MW00779060

Arthur Williams Rodenberger

Psalm 126:5

Joy in the Mourning

DEBORAH WILLIAMS RODENHIZER

Joy in the Mourning

a story of life after death

TATE PUBLISHING & *Enterprises*

Joy in the Mourning
Copyright © 2011 by Deborah Williams Rodenhizer All rights reserved.

No part of this publication may be reproduced, stored in a retrieval system or transmitted in any way by any means, electronic, mechanical, photocopy, recording or otherwise without the prior permission of the author except as provided by USA copyright law.

This book is designed to provide accurate and authoritative information with regard to the subject matter covered. This information is given with the understanding that neither the author nor Tate Publishing, LLC is engaged in rendering legal, professional advice. Since the details of your situation are fact dependent, you should additionally seek the services of a competent professional.

The opinions expressed by the author are not necessarily those of Tate Publishing, LLC.

Published by Tate Publishing & Enterprises, LLC
127 E. Trade Center Terrace | Mustang, Oklahoma 73064 USA
1.888.361.9473 | www.tatepublishing.com

Tate Publishing is committed to excellence in the publishing industry. The company reflects the philosophy established by the founders, based on Psalm 68:11,
"The Lord gave the word and great was the company of those who published it."

Book design copyright © 2011 by Tate Publishing, LLC. All rights reserved.
Cover design by Blake Brasor
Interior design by Nathan Harmony
Author photo by Tammy Williams

Published in the United States of America

ISBN: 978-1-61777-377-8
1. Self-Help / Death, Grief, Bereavement
2 Religion / Christian Life / Personal Growth
11.03.31

Dedication

This book is dedicated to my children: Christopher in heaven, Tom, Joe, Carrie, and Corinna. You all know how imperfect I am, but I hope that you also know that I have loved you from the depths of my being and will continue to do so forever.

And for my beautiful granddaughter, Cordelia—you are the balm that the Father used to soothe my soul and bring joy back into my life. Ama loves you so much!

Table of Contents

Introduction

I am not a professional writer, an expert on suicide, or a psychologist. I am just a woman who lost her son under the most tragic of circumstances and lived to tell the tale.

My heart's desire in writing this book is twofold. I want to help pastors, counselors, or any other person who is in a position to minister to those who have lost loved ones in a tragic way, and I want to help you to understand the feelings of those left behind and to be compassionate in dealing with them.

For those of you who have lost a loved one, my desire is to give you hope where there seems to be none and to tell you that there is indeed a light at the end of this pitch-black tunnel.

You *can* find comfort and relief for your pain. You *will* live on, and in doing so, you will carry the best of the person that you lost along with you.

I know this to be true, because I have survived the one thing I thought I could never survive. Once again, I can laugh, love, and find joy in life. There was a time when I thought it would be impossible to do so, and if it was possible, I didn't want to.

I will share my journey with you, along with what I have learned, and together we will find that there can be *Joy in the Mourning.*

Prologue

March 1, 2004, was a beautiful day. Blue skies and white fluffy clouds promised that spring was just around the corner. It was just an ordinary day. There was no sign that I would remember this day as the worst day of my life.

I was at work that afternoon when I had a surprise visit from my sister Marie and my niece, Maggie. We were enjoying our visit, as we always did, when the phone rang. It was our sister Jeanne, asking if I could leave a little early and stop by her house on the way home. When I told her that the girls had dropped by, she said to ask them to come too.

We thought nothing about it and followed each other to Jeanne's house. When we arrived, I saw that there were other family members' cars there. I began to feel fear in the pit of my stomach, and my immediate thought was that something was wrong with our mother, who lived with Jeanne and her family.

When we entered the house, I looked around for Mom. I saw her, and she seemed all right, but then I noticed that everyone else was crying. I quickly tried to determine who wasn't there.

The whole thing was surreal, and even though I don't have the best of memories, I can recount every detail of those first few minutes.

Jeanne came over to me and put her hands firmly on my shoulders, pushing me down onto an ottoman. She looked into my eyes and said the following words: "It's bad. It's Christopher. He's gone. He shot himself."

And thus began my journey into a mother's worst nightmare.

A Mother's Heart

A voice in Ramah, mourning and great weeping; Rachel weeping for her children and refusing to be comforted because her children are no more.

Jeremiah 31:15

Ever since I was a little girl, I wanted to be a mom. I had a lot of practice growing up. As the oldest of five children, I was often tasked with watching and helping with the younger ones. My dad was in the navy and often deployed, so you can imagine that my mom needed the help.

In addition to my brother and three sisters, I also watched younger ones at church or in the neighborhood. I asked for and received a doll for the first ten Christmases of my life.

I may have imagined doing other things in life, but being a mom was always at the top of the list. And of course, I believed that children would bring joy into my life and live on long after I died.

Christopher was the firstborn of my three sons. He was born in Norwich, Connecticut, on October 26, 1977. He was also the first grandchild on either side.

He was very much wanted and loved. He was followed by Tom on November 14, 1981, and Joe on December 11, 1986.

When I held Christopher for the first time, I felt the overwhelming responsibility that God had given me. I was terrified for a moment, and then I fell totally in love with this child.

Like my father, his father was in the navy and deployed for many months at a time. I lived eighteen hours away from my family, so it seemed as if, until his brothers came along, it was Christopher and me alone against the world.

He had ebony eyes, and when his hair finally came in, it was white-blond and curly. He received my grandmother's dimples and had the most beautiful smile.

Although he had colic (lactose intolerance, for the new generation), he was a good baby. He was sweet natured and fun to be with. He was a constant source of entertainment for my family and me. As the first child, grandchild, and nephew, we never tired of watching him.

I talked with him all the time, as I had very few others to talk to. Because I did, he had a firm grasp of the English language at a very early age. He also seemed to be an old soul, understanding things with wisdom beyond his years.

He loved nature and everything in God's creation (and I do mean everything).

Once, I found a dead minnow in his jeans pocket and another time watched him walk home with a snake in his hand. Being totally phobic about snakes, I had to intercept him before he brought it inside. He was adventurous and never seemed to fear anything.

It is hard to explain, but from an early age, he was often contemplative. That seems to be a strange word to use for a young child, but it was true. He seemed to see past this realm and into another. He had a strong will but was not given to tantrums.

He was never mean or cruel to others. He was protective of others, and he would always stand up for the underdog. This trait followed him through adulthood when he literally gave up his bed to someone who needed it and was content to sleep on the floor.

He had very high expectations of himself, and if he believed he couldn't do something well, he preferred not to try it at all. He was the classic underachiever, and it was often frustrating as a parent knowing that he was capable at excelling in any area he chose and then watching as he backed off, unwilling to be the focus of attention.

I wanted to tell you about Christopher as a person apart from the tragic circumstances that led to his death.

When we lose someone we love, we have a deep desire to talk about that person and to keep their memory alive. When our loved ones die as a result of suicide, drug overdose, or any other tragedy, there is also a desire to let people know the person apart from his or her actions.

These are our children, our parents, our nieces, and our nephews. They were loved and valued. That doesn't change because of an action or series of actions on their part.

After his death, I talked about Christopher all the time. I could bring him into almost every dialogue, no matter the topic. I could see that it often made people uncomfortable and, after a while, somewhat annoyed. But this was my son, whom I loved. He had many fine attributes, and I wanted him remembered for those and not for his death.

You can imagine how that made me feel. I could understand that because his death was a suicide it made others uncomfortable when I brought him up. I am sure that many had questions about the circumstances and reasons for his death. They didn't feel right about asking, so it was easier to not talk about him.

If they had only understood my need to keep him with me and to remind people that he was a wonderful human being who had a purpose in life. One of the most important things that friends and family can do is let the survivors talk about their loved one as often and in any way they need to.

This can go a long way in helping them to heal. Be a safe place for them to share. Express interest in hearing their hearts. Share memories of your own, and confirm the value of that person.

There are not enough pages to write everything about my son, but I did want you to know some things about him.

I want you to know him for who he was, not how or why he died. I want you to know that I loved him and love him still.

Christopher's Story

I tell you the truth, unless a kernel of wheat falls
to the ground and dies, it remains only a single
seed. But if it dies, it produces many seeds.

John 12:24

On Monday, March 1, 2004, Christopher went to work.
Nobody seemed to notice anything out of the ordinary.
At lunchtime, he went home and ended his life.

It was such a shock, and I didn't have enough
information to make sense of what I was hearing.
After his death, and over a period of time, I was able
to find some pieces to this puzzle. Christopher had
met with his brother Tom a week before he died and

related some details that he had kept to himself for fifteen years.

It seems that Christopher had been the victim of a violent sexual assault by two older boys when he was about nine years old. He never told us because they had threatened to do "even worse" to his younger brother Tom if he did.

I was devastated by this news, of course. This news was almost as terrible to hear as the news of his death. How could this happen to my child and I not know about it? I felt that I was a horrible parent not to have known and because my son felt that he had to suffer alone in this horror.

I began to think back through the years to see if I could find evidence of his suffering. I was able to recall how his behavior changed about that time. He was also entering into puberty, and I thought the changes were reflective of that part of his growing up. He was my first child, and so I was naïve about a lot of things back then.

He began to keep more to himself and became somewhat sullen at times. It's not that I never asked him what was troubling him; it's just that he would never tell me. I assumed that it was normal not to want to tell your mom everything, so I kept an eye on him, but I never suspected the truth.

This knowledge, of course, led to me blaming myself for not uncovering the secret and getting him the help he needed. But he never exhibited any obvious signs of anxiety or emotional trauma. He was very good at keeping things to himself.

He was never a problem at home or in school. He was practiced at flying under the radar. He had friends and enjoyed normal things. He was a normal older brother to Tom and Joe.

I eventually remembered some conversations we had over the years. At age twelve, he had his first real crush, and when she didn't return the feelings, he seemed to have more than the normal angst over it. I remember him telling me that no one would ever love him. When I asked him why he thought such a thing, he told me that I could never understand.

He would also talk about never wanting to have children. I found that strange because he liked and was good with kids. He was adamant about it, making comments about not wanting to bring children into such a horrible world.

These things make sense to me now, but taken by themselves—without the knowledge of what had happened to him—they still seem like normal growing pains and statements made by a teen or preteen.

The story of your loved one may be similar or totally different. One thing they all have in common is that they were suffering in ways we could never know and they couldn't see an end to it any other way.

Christopher went on to find the love of his life. He began dating Carrie in 1997, and they were married three years later. They had gone to high school together, but it was Christopher's best friend who set them up on their first date.

He was very happy during this time, and I believed that whatever had been bothering him was now in the past. He held jobs, was responsible, and spent time with friends and family. But again, there were things I did not know.

Carrie was Christopher's best friend as well as his wife. She later related to me things that showed how much he struggled in the last year of his life. She suffered alone during this time, as she felt that she couldn't betray him by telling us when he asked her not to, but she was often terrified of what she witnessed.

This is Carrie's story, and I will not try to tell it. And though we have walked different paths in our pain and grief and each have our own regrets, we were united in our understanding of the evil that lay behind Christopher's torment.

We also had a united front when planning the funeral. We wanted it to be a celebration of his life and an opportunity to share the gospel with those who needed to hear it. Many that were in attendance were the friends that Christopher had tried to lead to the truth.

As John 12:24 states, a harvest can come from a single seed dying. We saw six people come to salvation at the funeral. Christopher shared his faith in the last two years of his life, and he shared it again through his death.

Making that our focus helped Carrie and me through a most difficult time, and I believe God gave us supernatural strength as well, because we made that our goal. We refused to let Satan have any victory at all.

The Bible tells us that what Satan intends for evil, God will use for good. The enemy sought to destroy Christopher, and though he succeeded in tormenting him and driving him to his death, he did not win. He could not take Christopher's soul, and we refused to let him take over our emotions or actions during this time.

The Bible tells us that God knows the number of our days. This understanding came slowly to me, but it did come. If I believe that God creates each one of us, has a specific purpose for us, and knows the number of the days of our life, I have to also believe that God knew when he would allow Christopher to come home.

I know that many of you struggle with this as well. As his mother, that day would always come too soon. These loved ones will always be our child, our friend, or our spouse. Death doesn't change that. How they died doesn't change that.

In accepting that God is sovereign and that nothing happens apart from his divine will, we can be comforted, but it can also be disconcerting . His will rarely aligns with our desires and how we think things should be.

I had to learn to trust his sovereignty and in his perfect love in order to move on from this event and in order to let him heal my shattered heart.

$\mathcal{A}$ Trail of Victims

Remember that my life is but breath; my eye
shall not again see good.

Job 7:7

According to the World Health Organization, over
one million people will commit suicide each year.
That is one every forty seconds.

In the 105 reporting countries, suicide is the third
leading cause of death for people aged fifteen to
thirty-five years old.

It is never easy when someone we love dies. We
still feel the pain of loss even when our older loved
ones die and it has been expected.

When that person dies by his or her own hand or as a result of choices he or she has made, the death brings with it so many other emotions: pain, guilt, blame, and shame.

There is more than one victim in a suicide. The collateral damage can be devastating to families and relationships. The same can be said in the cases of drug overdose, car accidents, and murder.

There is also a stigma attached to suicide that adds to the difficulty already faced by those left behind. Many Christians still believe that suicide is the unpardonable sin. Others feel that those close to the victim should have been able to prevent their deaths.

For almost everyone, suicide is, at best, an extremely uncomfortable topic. It may cause trouble for those close to the family in knowing how to approach them or even if they should approach them.

It could be that your loved one didn't die by his own hand but under circumstances in which blame could be placed by others. Your situation could be different than mine, but it could involve similar situations that are difficult to handle—perhaps a traffic accident or a drug overdose in which the actions of your loved one played a part in his or her death.

As a mother, I needed to know what had gone wrong. It is a very strong part of my personality as well. I have always wanted to know about and understand everything about a situation before accepting it.

Sometimes an event or series of events occur in a person's life that will lay the groundwork for emotional distress later on. I also believe that a person's personality and emotional makeup play a part in choices that they make and in how they respond to traumatic or stressful events.

I was not at all bothered by friends wanting to help me find answers to my questions. You can tell when a person is genuinely concerned and when they are being critical or pious in their comments.

For me, some of the most difficult times came unexpectedly. I could be walking down an aisle in a store and become angry that people around me were carrying on as if this monumental event hadn't taken place. I hated Mother's Day. I would start crying at the most inappropriate times.

And then there was the feeling of being responsible. Overwhelming guilt would begin to flood my soul. And the fear for my other sons, Tom and Joe, would steal any peace that might have been attained.

Maybe there were things we could have done or said differently, but in all likelihood, those things would not, in and of themselves, change the outcome.

Don't be afraid to help the survivors find answers, if that is what they want to do. But be aware that this is their loved one and it is normal for them to be defensive with anyone who seems to cast judgment. Finding answers in order to understand and find closure is different than looking for where to cast blame.

In the end, finding some of the answers did help me to find closure. That is not to say that the answers made sense of this tragedy. Those left behind will never believe that their loved one's death makes sense. But in the case of suicide, understanding the events that led up to the decision may help us to accept that our love one was in extreme pain. Understanding their pain can help us to forgive them and release them, and that becomes necessary for our own healing.

At times, I would feel the need to gather every memory of Christopher that I could, like pieces of a puzzle that I was compelled to complete. Finding these pieces did help me to understand, but to be truthful, whatever answers I found could not and would not ever justify his death to me. In fact, some of them were very painful to accept. He was hurting and tormented. It didn't matter what caused it. As a mother, I would have wanted to help him or, in the extreme, protect him from those things.

Christopher was my child. I loved him dearly, and I love him still. I am glad that I have twenty-six years of memories and pictures documenting his life. I do not regret one day of his life or one day of mine as his mother.

Nothing he could do would ever change that. It breaks my heart that he was hurting. I know that any of you who are parents would understand this. We would gladly exchange our lives for those of our children. We would gladly accept all of the pain and the hurt to prevent them from suffering.

But each person has their own life and must live it themselves. We cannot live it for them. We cannot protect them from evil or suffering. We can only love them and be there for them unconditionally. It is always up to them to reach out and accept what is offered.

This is a bold truth that I have learned and finally accepted. As God himself is grieved by our pain and suffering, we too are grieved at the suffering of our children.

Beauty from Ashes

Those who sow in tears will reap in joy.
Psalm 126:5

Even though Christopher had shared his resolve about not having children, God had other plans. I found out that I was to be a grandmother for the first time in the fall of 2003. I was ecstatic, and Christopher and Carrie seemed happy too.

When Christopher died, Carrie was five and a half months pregnant. Caring for this child—the last remnant of our Christopher—became the top priority of my life. Not only was she part of him, but I also felt that it was my responsibility to step into this role on his behalf. Cordelia Isabella Parrilla Rodenhizer was born on June 15, 2004.

As you can imagine, it was a very emotional experience. My sister Marie was the attending midwife, and she had briefed the hospital on the situation. They were very accommodating to us out of sensitivity to our circumstances.

Carrie ended up having fifty-six hours of labor, trying valiantly to deliver naturally, and then ended up having a C-section. The hospital staff allowed both Carrie's mom and me into the operating room. While Esther comforted her daughter, they allowed me to carry Cordelia to the nursery.

As I held that child in my arms, I felt many emotions at once. I remember thinking that if Christopher had just held on long enough to see this child, he would have decided to stay forever.

I also thought, with great sadness, about this beautiful child growing up without her father. Bittersweet is an apt description for the emotions running through me at that time.

I have been blessed to help care for this child for the first five years of her life. She is a perfect blend of her two parents. She is not fatherless. We know that

God is "Father to the fatherless," [citation] and he has been faithful in fulfilling that role.

We have not had the discussion with Cordie about the details of her dad's death. We have told her all along that her dad is in heaven. Whenever the topic of heaven comes up, she will simply tell you that her daddy is there with Jesus.

In September, 2009, she and I had a phone conversation. This is how it went:

> "Ama, I have some seeds."
>
> "That's great, Cords! Are you going to plant them?"
>
> "Yep, and you know what, Ama? Maybe it will be a giant beanstalk, and we can climb it all the way up to heaven and see my daddy!"
>
> "Cordie, if that beanstalk starts to grow, you call Ama, and we'll climb it together!"

Seeing things through her eyes has really helped me keep things in perspective. We could all learn from those with a pure, childlike faith. She accepts that God loves her and that her daddy is in heaven. She accepts those of us in her life as her family, and she sees it as complete.

Carrie is an excellent mom and has done an incredible job of raising Cordie. She is an incredible kid, and I have no doubt that she will be important to the world and to God's kingdom.

Cordie has been a healing balm to my heart. In her, we have a part of Christopher with us, but aside from that, the child is pure joy.

She is like her dad in that she seems to have a mature spiritual understanding. She is also very loving and kind. Like her dad, she ministers to others and hates to see anyone hurting.

She has given my family something positive to focus on. There have been times for all of us when it was tempting to give up and give in to our pain. We would think of this child and, with renewed determination, get back up and fight.

It has been our joy and honor to be used by God to shelter, teach, and love this child as she grows into the woman that God has created her to be.

I am excited to see how he will use her. We are vigilant over her physical, emotional, and spiritual wellbeing. But we also allow God to continue to bring us joy through this beautiful child.

We know that God created her for his own purposes, but he gave us a gift in placing her with our family. There are many ways to honor our loved ones or to make sure that a part of them lives on. We have planted trees in Christopher's name to honor the part of him that loved nature. We have purchased Bibles in his honor to be given to those who desire them.

Think about your loved one, their character and what they loved. Create memorials or legacies to them in your own unique way. This brings healing and helps us to concentrate on the good things about their time on earth. It helps to know that a part of them remains.

A Strange Fraternity

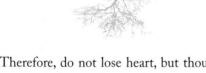

Therefore, do not lose heart, but though our outer man is decaying our inner man is being renewed day by day.

2 Corinthians 4:16

Something that can help some survivors of suicide or other tragic losses is to hear stories of other victims. I found a website where friends and family of those lost to suicide could post pictures and stories about their loved ones. For some, it might sound morbid, but I was desperate to connect with others in this exclusive and horrifying club. As I read their stories, I felt less alone, and I also felt that Christopher was not unique in experiencing what he had.

I remember so many powerful emotions running through me while I was doing this. Their pain was my pain, and it brought me comfort somehow. By reading their stories and seeing their pictures, I was helping to validate their lives and identify with their loved one's pain at losing them.

There is no *right* way to do this. You simply do what you need to do and whatever helps you feel that you aren't so isolated in your pain.

People in your normal circle may be so uncomfortable with the issue that you end up feeling alone. Even family members have a different way of dealing with their grief. My own sons were often uncomfortable when I brought Christopher into almost every conversation in the beginning. I could see that it brought fresh pain to their eyes, so I became self-conscious about it and tried to be considerate of their need to grieve in their own way.

I had two other sons to worry about during this time. In the years following Christopher's death, Tom and Joe went through some horrible times. It had a devastating effect on both of them. This was their older brother that they looked up to and almost idealized.

It was necessary for me to pay close attention to them during this time. I'll admit that the enemy tried his best to keep me in fear of losing one or both of them as well. I put my own grief on hold many times in those years to try to fight for my other two children. I was being vigilant and thought I could do for them what I hadn't been able to do for Christopher.

Men handle their grief differently than women do. In order to move on, they seem to have a need to put the event in a box and not look at it. Sometimes they even walk away from any reminders of their loss, even if those reminders are their other children or family members who seem to be a constant reminder of the tragedy they are trying to forget.

Women have a need and desire to talk and share their grief. This can cause problems in a marriage or between parents and their surviving children who are of the opposite sex. This difference in handling grief can place a wedge between family members.

Finding others who understand is a great benefit. I never went to a support group, but doing so would be a fine way of sharing your grief and listening to those who might be further ahead on their road to healing.

I was blessed to have a small, close set of friends and family who allowed me to talk when I needed to. They also prayed night and day for me, and that was important because I could not pray for myself.

I was a member of a church during this time. It is a difficult thing to say, but the church did not minister to my un-churched sons or me during this nightmare. I was told that it was the responsibility of a person's Sunday school class (or small group) to minister to their needs. Since I was not a part of a class at that time, there was no one to minister to me.

I find this disconcerting, to say the least. I was not part of a small group because I couldn't find one where I felt I connected or fit into. My sons were not attending church, so they had no group to see to their needs.

The church often misses the boat in ministering to members of their congregations. Those that are hurting need the love of Christ the most. We spend far too much time, money, and effort into creating programs and pageantry and not enough in ministering to the hearts and souls of our own community.

I believe the Bible teaches (in the example of the early church) that we are to first see to the needs of the church body and then to evangelize and meet the needs of others. The church is full of hurting and imperfect people. If we do not minister healing to each other, we will not be able to minister outside of the church.

I will admit that I developed a resentful attitude about this in the first several years. After much prayer and self-reflection, I felt that God wanted me to confess these feelings, ask forgiveness, and perhaps help the pastors and those in church leadership to understand the situation so that others would not be hurt.

So I made an appointment to meet with my pastors. I confessed my bitter feelings and asked their forgiveness. I then tried to explain to them what had happened and how concerned I was that others might be hurt in the future if things did not change.

That is when they explained to me that the small groups (Sunday school/Connection classes) had the responsibility to meet those needs.

If you are a pastor or a church counselor, I ask you to seek out answers to this problem. I believe there should always be someone in the church who could see that those who are suffering or hurting have what they need and are cared for by the church. Not doing this could cause those people to resent and stay away from the one place that they need to be.

I began to search the Internet for others that were a part of this horrible fraternity. I felt a real need to connect with others who could really understand what I was going through.

Being there for others is a great way to pull through your own grief. I haven't counseled many other survivors of suicide, but friends and acquaintances have been given my permission to give my phone number to anyone who needs it. I have walked this road before them and would be honored to walk with them, if needed.

I have counseled others in grief over losing someone to other forms of death. My son died through suicide, but I would be grieving his loss no matter how it happened. Helping others with their grief has helped me a great deal. In some ways, it redeems Christopher's death to me. It becomes a tool that can be used for God's purposes and thwarts the enemy's plan of destruction.

That's a key element to this for me. I believe strongly that we battle good and evil on a daily basis.

I also believe that victims of suicide are under a very strong demonic attack. Therefore, we need to counter that evil with good at every opportunity. Otherwise, evil continues to win.

Love and Support

My intercessor is my friend as my eyes pour
out tears to God.

Job 16:20

It is important to us for others to know that our loved
ones should not be defined by what they did but by
who they were. It is also helpful to understand that as
close as we might have been, no one can ever know
exactly what is inside another person.

Survivors are victims too. We often feel the need
to assume blame, but the truth is we are victims of
another's choice or circumstances beyond our control.
We are the ones left behind in pain and without those

whom we loved. In the end, they may have believed that they were somehow protecting us or sparing us some pain by ending their life, but this was a lie straight from the pit.

It is difficult to allow ourselves to think this way. We feel that if we refuse blame or even talk about our own pain, we are being insensitive to the one who died. This is simply not true. We can never find healing if we feel guilty about admitting that we need it.

We need to speak and hear truth in order to heal and be set free. If we don't believe this, then we will be caught in the same web of lies that our loved ones were.

Survivors of suicide or any other tragic death are left with a tremendous amount of pain. But next to that are the many, many questions we have. We will lie awake at night and try to find pieces of this puzzle. For me, the need to understand what happened was imperative. Without it, I could not allow myself to move forward into the healing process.

Now, not every survivor feels this way. Some do not want to know what was going on inside the person and may find it terrorizing to relive the victim's pain or even a dishonor to the victim to pry into his or her very personal feelings, especially when they had worked so hard to keep their torment a secret.

We may be afraid of what will discover. It is not an easy thing to do.

Even though I was almost obsessed at times with finding out the reasons that he committed suicide, I did not want to know the details of Christopher's death for a long time. Over the following months, I would ask my sister Jeanne about the details. She was the one who dealt directly with the police and was the keeper of the facts about that day.

She would gauge whether I was truly at a place where I could hear the details and then would carefully but truthfully answer my questions. It was extremely helpful to have her assume this role.

I know how devastating Christopher's death was to her. In her part of his eulogy, she shared with everyone how she had always felt that she and Christopher were soul mates and understood each other in ways that others couldn't. She was grieving as well, but she put that aside to be there for me when I needed her.

Since she has a master's in counseling and a personality that is more geared to logic than emotion, she graciously took on the role. I will be eternally grateful to her for that.

If you are a pastor or counselor, then you could be of great help to the survivors in seeing that there is someone in this role of spokesperson and handling details that are too difficult for most of the immediate family to handle at this time.

There were others who helped me during this time. I had many friends praying for us. Prayer places us before the throne of God and covers us in protection. My boss and board of directors gave me the time off that I needed in order to take care of the funeral details and to deal with my grief and the grief of my family.

My mom and my siblings ministered to me as well. I have mentioned the part that Jeanne played. She also allowed Christopher's wife, Carrie, to move in with her family and my mom. My sister Edie and her husband, Reg, went over to the house and retrieved Carrie's things and took care of cleaning up the aftermath. I can't even begin to imagine the supernatural, emotional strength that God gave them to do that.

My brother, Raymond, picked up and notified our youngest son, Joe. He would hold me and let me cry when I needed to. I always knew that I could go to him if I needed to, even though his heart was breaking as well.

My sister Marie and my mom were always a comfort to me. They never judged Christopher or me, and they loved me through those dark times. Mom helped financially with the funeral. Christopher was her first grandchild, and I know that his death devastated her.

Christopher's death hit all of them hard too. But they put aside their own pain to help my children and me get through.

My friend Sheryl and her son drove from Florida to North Carolina to stay with me. They stayed for about ten days. She kept an eye on me, making sure that I ate, etc., and she encouraged me to journal during this time. She also ran interference for me when people would call or stop by. She protected me from decisions or encounters that I was in no shape to deal with.

I felt that I needed to do something tangible to reflect moving forward, so she and Aaron helped me paint my great room and kitchen area a soothing, earthy green. The paint is there to this day. It symbolizes new life and the nature that Christopher loved so much. I have never grown tired of it.

Sometimes you have to make changes that reflect moving forward. If it helps to change your look or your environment, go ahead. Do what you need to do. Do not be afraid that in changing things that you will be removing your loved one's memories.

For me, it was a way of arranging my space to reflect the best memories of Christopher, as well as new life and moving forward. I often felt as if I were drowning in my grief or locked in a room in which there was no outlet.

Rearranging my environment gave me a sense that I could move forward and keep the good memories and feelings intact while ridding myself of the horrible thoughts about his death. It gave me something tangible to do and helped to empower me when I had felt so powerless.

You may find different ways for doing this. You need to find your own path out of the maze. With God's help and direction, you will be able to do this. The key is not to stop where you are.

The Desert

I will even make a roadway in the wilderness,
rivers in the desert.

Isaiah 43:19b (NASB)

Jeanne once told me that if I found myself in a desert, the one thing I should never do is stop. She said that when you stop in the desert, you will surely die.

When we find ourselves in the desert of grieving, we will come to a point of wanting to do just that: stop, lie down, and quit. It just seems too difficult, and our grief has drained all of our energy .

There are stages of grief: denial, guilt, anger, bargaining, and acceptance. You can get stuck in any of the first four and never arrive at the last one.

These stages of grief are normal and even helpful to our healing. We take them in our own time and in no particular order.

I went through the anger stage fairly early on. Carrie went through that stage more recently. It is uncomfortable to be angry with someone that you are in grief over losing. But it is necessary, and it is an honest emotion.

Christopher had left us dealing with the aftermath of his suicide. I resented that. I had to watch my other children and family members suffer this tragedy; he did not. And although I knew that he was not totally in control of himself at the end, he was responsible because he did not come to us. He did not seek help. He made a choice.

I could not lie to myself, so I let myself feel that emotion until I felt the time was right to release it and to fully forgive Christopher.

Many get stuck in the guilt stage. This stage can do some damage along the way. I have seen many almost destroyed by guilt. Most of the guilt is unwarranted, but the person is so overtaken with it that he or she cannot see that truth.

When you find yourself in one of these deserts, do not stop. Do not lie down and give up. Your freedom is just on the other side, so you must push through.

Find someone to help you. It should be someone who is spiritually mature, emotionally safe for you, and maybe even someone who has experience with deserts of their own.

Do not be ashamed to admit that you're stuck. Never be ashamed to ask for help. God designed us for community so that we have to rely on each other.

I guarantee that there is a new life and a new joy waiting on the other side.

Spiritual Truth

He will swallow up death forever. The Sovereign Lord will wipe away the tears from all faces; He will remove the disgrace of His people from all the earth.

Isaiah 25:8

The spiritual aspect of this topic is a key component in understanding and accepting the things that are happening to us. If you are a believer, then you know that, from the foundation of the world and even before, there was a major revolt in heaven. This revolt resulted in Satan and his demons warring against God the Father and Jesus the Son. He was cast out of heaven and allowed to reign here for a time, seeking to distort God's truth and destroy everything he loves.

Basic Christianity, yes, but hear me out. As Christians, we say that we know and believe the doctrine and the Scriptures, but when we go through a time of testing in our lives, we find out how much we really know and if we really believe what we think we do.

I was raised in a Baptist home, saved at a Billy Graham crusade, and was in church without fail for the first nineteen years of my life. I thought I knew what I believed. I had never questioned the things I had been taught. I never went through a there-is-no-God phase.

But I did go off on my own, thinking I knew enough to keep myself on the track to my heavenly home. I stopped going to church, stopped the daily Bible readings, and flirted with the world's many delights. Like so many others who were raised in church, I had felt stifled and wanted to go out, find myself, and experience all the world had to offer. I saw no danger, only excitement ahead. After all, I was safe, wasn't I? And of course, I wasn't as bad as some people, and there were paths that I would never consider going down. I knew what I was doing. Uh-huh ...

Even though I didn't throw out what I was taught, I did, on occasion, try to mix in various other things, like tarot cards, Native American spirituality, etc. I watered down my Christianity and, in doing so, opened myself up to the enemy.

After many years of living like that, God finally confronted me on what it was that I really wanted and whom I really served. He spoke about it being time to get off the fence and truly make a choice. I was amazed to find out that it wasn't enough to just believe. In making choices every moment of every day, I was declaring my choice—my way or God's way. Evidently you can't straddle the fence forever.

By that time, I had realized that I hadn't done such a great job of running things. My marriage fell apart, I lost my job, and I was frankly miserable. I was also scared and very tired. I repented and consecrated myself to live out my faith and turned my life over to the One who could do something with it. And from January 1997 on, that is exactly what I did. Of course, I have stumbled down the path at times, but at least I was finally and firmly on the right road.

Now, I have given that bit of my background so that you can understand where I was spiritually. By

2004, I had been on this path for a while, and I had had to relearn things. My Christianity had been a part of my life, just as my siblings have the same gene pool. It just was. But living the Christian life with Jesus at the helm is a whole different story.

I had to be tested along the way. Going through trials and being tested proves what we know and teaches us to apply that knowledge. It gives us a chance to let God prove himself and tests the truth of his Word. The testing strengthens our faith and opens our eyes to see beyond this life and these circumstances.

From January 1997 through the early months of 2004, I was learning the deeper truths behind the Scripture and gaining new understanding about what following Christ really meant. It looked nothing like the life I had previously lived. I knew this was important. This life was full of experiences that became either victories for Satan or victories for Christ. There really was no middle ground.

I was also learning about *crucifixion of the flesh* and *suffering with Christ*. It certainly hadn't been about me at all, and it was never supposed to be easy.

I had a long way to go, but now I know why God had me choose sides four years before. Since I had been studying, learning, and trying to grow in my faith and my spiritual knowledge, he was able to prepare me to seek his help when I would need it most. He was teaching me what I would need to know. He knew what was coming, even though I did not.

Christopher had been a Christian for two and a half years before he died. I know he struggled for years with the demons that tormented him. In fact, I remember him telling me that he could never be a Christian but that I would never understand why, so he never tried to explain it to me. I later found out that the enemy told him that he could never be worthy and that he belonged to Satan. Of course, I knew Satan was lying to him, so I continued to pray.

When he became a Christian, he was not exempt from torment. In fact, I believe it became worse because Satan knew that Christopher was now aligned with his enemy. He had a target on his back. But since Christopher had trouble with traditional church and most of his friends were unsaved, he unfortunately didn't learn how important it was to surround yourself with other believers, to be transparent and have others praying for you. This opened him up to a very difficult time of spiritual warfare, and he tried to carry these burdens on his own.

For those of you who are not believers, you may not understand or even believe everything that I am saying. But let me tell you, it's the only thing that makes any sense to me, and believe me, I have had some experience in trying to find the truth in many different areas. I have never found a better explanation of good and evil and why such terrible things happen on this earth as the one found in the Word of God.

God is good, Satan is evil, and they are at war with each other. We are the prize.

Satan wants to torment, control, and ultimately destroy each person because God created us for himself so that we could love him, fellowship with him, and spend eternity with him. Satan lost his place and hates us for being the object of God's love and attention. He also wants to rule us, play us, and trick us into believing lies about God so he can take us away from him.

Satan has demons (fallen angels) that are at his command. They hate us too. You know how misery loves company. God has his angels at his command. They serve us and protect because God orders them to.

We are in a war. Every day. If we don't understand this, then it will be harder to comprehend what happens in our lives and the lives of others. And we will not be prepared to fight back or survive the attacks.

I believe that those people we love who choose suicide (or drug and alcohol abuse) are tormented by demons. I hold Satan 100 percent accountable for my son's death. He is the author of everything evil. He is death and destruction. All the anger and rage I felt, I directed at him.

What helped me get through this time was understanding who God was and who Satan was. I knew that God loved Christopher, even more than I did. And I knew that he loved me. So I let God love me and carry me through, and I focused all of my blame and hatred on the true enemy, Satan.

This is important to understand because those of us left behind will begin to assign blame on ourselves or onto others. As humans, we need someone to blame. This can add to the devastation that has already been inflicted. Many marriages do not survive an event like this. Many families begin to divide, and many of the family members begin to feel that they are secondary to the one who has died.

And perhaps the most common one to blame is God. He is all-powerful and could have intervened, after all. He could have healed the person from his or her pain. He sees and knows everything that we cannot. It seems to make the most sense to blame God.

If you understand the scenario that I previously laid out—that God is good and Satan is evil—you begin to see the truth about what lies behind this horror. Satan is the great liar, deceiver, and destroyer. There is no evil in God, and he sacrificed himself to bring all of mankind back to him.

As a believer, this becomes the greatest test of what you always thought you believed. At some point, you have to decide whom you are going to listen to.

Even though I drew close to God during this time, I was not immune to the attacks of the enemy. I often resented that people were going on with their lives as if nothing at all had occurred. For me, the world had turned upside down, and it seemed a mockery of me when I would see others laughing and enjoying life.

I was tempted to turn bitter and angry. I couldn't celebrate holidays. Mother's Day was torment for me. I refused to decorate my house for the holidays.

I had to push through these feelings. The feelings, in and of themselves, were not wrong. But I could not let myself continue to walk in them. If I wanted to heal and move forward, I could not let myself be mired down in my grief and self-pity.

I also wanted to use what I had learned for others' benefit. I had to model faith to my sons and to others. I was determined that the enemy would not create any more casualties.

When we allow God to direct our steps and use our circumstance for his purposes, we snatch the victory from the enemy. We change from victims to victors.

Godly Encounters

It will also come to pass that before they call,
I will answer; and while they are speaking, I
will hear.

Isaiah 65:24

During the ten days following Christopher's death,
God blessed me with many spiritual encounters. Up
until that day, I had never experienced such a powerful, spiritual, and personal time with God. I have not
experienced any since then.

I know that God, in his love for me, allowed these
times with him in order to personally minister heal-

ing to me. There are times that I long to have such an encounter again.

The following is an illustration of one such encounter.

On the night Christopher died, I reluctantly went to bed. Although exhausted, I was afraid I would never be able to sleep. As I lay there, I began to speak to God.

> Me: "I will only ask you one question, and it is this: Why did you not intervene?"
>
> God: "Do you trust me?"
>
> Me: "Yes, but you have not answered my question."
>
> God: "*Do you trust me?*"
>
> Me: "*Yes!*"
>
> God: "Do you really trust me?"
>
> Me: "Why are you asking me this? You know that I trust you! Haven't I given up everything to follow you? I know that I'm not perfect, but haven't I been trying my best to grow and learn?"
>
> God: "I too know what it's like to lose a son."
>
> Me: "Yes, yes, you do."
>
> God: "If you really trust me and you want me to help you, then let go, and let me carry you."

I thought I trusted him. I was talking to him and asking him to help me, but he seemed to be asking me to go farther than my mind was able to go. I had to think of a way to release myself in order to reach out to God completely. I didn't know how to do this.

So I closed my eyes and visualized my two hands hanging from a bar of some sort. I pictured each finger slowly releasing its hold. When the last finger left the bar, I fell into a deep, dreamless sleep. I was resting in him.

The next ten days were surreal for me. Everything looked different, and my perception was heightened. I was totally aware of what was happening, but the horror and pain of Christopher's death weren't penetrating and devastating me.

I believe I was experiencing what it is truly like to be carried by God himself and, in a supernatural way, to go through the fire without being burned.

It enabled me to get through and help plan the funeral and all of those necessary things that had to be done. It gave me the strength to help my family through their pain.

God showed me many things during this time, and I know what a blessing it was to have this special time with him. I have longed for it many times in the last six years.

On another night, I couldn't sleep. I went into a spare bedroom and sat down by the window. It was a clear night, and I sat there, looking up at the stars. "Help me to see and to understand," I said.

In the next instant, I was taken up and seemed to be flying high among the stars. Someone was on my right, supporting me. I didn't see as much as sense that it was Jesus himself.

He told me that he wanted me to see something. Below us seemed to be a floating ribbon. It dipped and floated as ribbons do. It was purple in color. Suddenly, we began to descend rapidly toward the ribbon. As we drew closer, I was able to see various times and events in Christopher's life. There was his birth, his smile as a toddler, etc.

We would dip in close, see a short clip, and then rise back up again. We continued this process until the last scene, which was the funeral. The scene I saw was when the six individuals accepted the invitation to salvation that was offered by our pastor.

We began to fly away from the ribbon, and I was placed back into the room. All of a sudden, I realized that Christopher's life was complete. He had served his purpose. I also knew that everything in his life meant something. His death came too soon for me, but not for God.

This was a gift to me, and it also allowed God to be able to speak truths to me in ways that I would be receptive. He showed me things that I needed to see and understand in order to survive this but, most importantly, also so I could encourage others.

A week or so after the funeral, my family informed me that they wanted to do something special for my fiftieth birthday the following month. They said that, considering the circumstances, they would like to send me on an all-expenses-paid trip anywhere I wanted to go.

They told me that I could take my friend Sheryl with me, so the two of us decided on Maui. My grandchild was due in June, so we decided to wait until August to go.

I had not traveled outside of the US since I was a child. I also had a phobia about flying. One of the miraculous things God did for me during this time was deliver me from my fears and allow me to get on that airplane.

He reminded me that he had brought me through the worst thing that I could imagine and that all of my fears and phobias were nothing compared to losing my child. When confronted with the worst things in life, we suddenly realize how petty our fears are.

So I boarded that plane, and after many hours, I landed on the beautiful island of Maui. I knew that God had provided this gift for me through my family. I went, expecting him to speak to me during this week and to come home with a clear idea about how he would use me in the years ahead.

I was convinced that he wanted me to use my experiences to help and to minister to others, so I brought along the journal that I had begun (at my friend's suggestion) and planned to record everything he said to me.

I'll be honest and tell you that I never heard one word from him. I received no plans or instructions. I left without words of knowledge. But let me tell you what he did instead.

I woke each morning and had my coffee on the patio, watching beautiful sunrises.

After that, I would dress and walk down to the beach. As I walked, I would beg God to speak to me. I asked him to show me his heart.

Every day on that beautiful island, I would find a heart-shaped rock. I am not kidding you! Each day, I would look down and discover heart-shaped lava rocks and some shells worn down from the ocean until they took on that same shape.

I collected one each day and brought them home with me. I understood that God gave me that week in order to refresh me and to love on me.

I saw his love in the sunrises and sunsets and in his awesome creation. I knew that he loved me enough to place heart-shaped rocks as a tangible symbol of that love.

I am nothing special. What God did for me, he will do for you. He takes no pleasure in our suffering. He weeps with us in our pain. I believe he cried for Christopher in a way that even his mother could not do.

I understand verses in the Bible in a new way now. All of those "suffering" verses and verses about "trials and tribulations" purifying us and bringing us closer to Christlikeness are in there for a reason. It is a painful truth but still a truth. In our suffering, we gain understanding and develop a life that looks more like Christ's.

It's amazing how much we think we believe and think we know about God and his relationship with his creation. It is only through the trials and the fires of life that you find out. The fire will truly burn off all but the core of what is in your heart. When you discover what trusting God really means, it looks quite different than you thought it would.

And the part about submitting to his will over our own? It comes with a price, but I have found that it's the only way to survive, to move forward and live again.

God created Christopher and knew the number of his days. I was honored to be chosen to be his mother and to raise him, but he was never mine to begin with.

We think we are in control of our lives and that we have the capability to control the lives of our children. We think we can protect them from evil and from harm. And I really thought God and I had an understanding—he would never take my children from me.

In reality, we do not have the power to protect our children from everything. It is impossible to escape pain and suffering in this life.

In accepting that God is in control and that he loves us in a greater way than we will ever be capable of understanding, I was able to truly trust him and let him move me forward, knowing that he had a plan. And even though Christopher was only twenty-six at the time of his death, I believe he had accomplished his purpose here on earth.

But the greatest comfort that I had at that time and have to this day is the knowledge that I will see him again one day and that he is free from his suffering, basking in the love of his Savior.

So you can see why my spiritual belief system is vital to the healing I experienced. I cannot give you hope without it. I know no other truth than this. None of the other religions, magic, or philosophies could help me.

If you are a believer, then you have access to all of this too. You just need to find a way to release everything to God and let him truly carry you. You must be willing to acknowledge that he is Lord and his will is more important than your own.

It goes against our human, selfish will to do this. We think that we let him lead and that we trust him, but in times like these, we find out how small our faith is.

If you are not a follower of Christ, I can assure you that he and he alone is your hope. He is God's Son, who was willingly sacrificed so that we could come back to him. None of us would willingly give up our children, especially for those who would never accept the gift or who would spit in our face for doing so.

But God loves in a different way than we do. His love is pure and selfless. He proved that he would do anything to bring us back to him. He will not interfere with our rights to choose. He gave us freewill, after all. But his main desire is to be reconciled to us.

I also believe that God gives everyone, and I mean without exception, every opportunity to come to him. If you do not know for sure that your loved one had made that choice, I can only comfort you by saying that only God knows what happens in the last seconds before death. And since I believe in what I have shared with you, I can only believe that if they reached out to God, they found him reaching right back.

Closing Thoughts

Provide for those who grieve in Zion—to bestow on them a crown of beauty instead of ashes, the oil of gladness instead of mourning and a garment of praise instead of a spirit of despair.
Isaiah 61:3

Carrie told me a story once that has stayed with me and helped me keep the proper perspective. She said that shortly after Christopher's death, someone said something along the lines of knowing that she wished Christopher were still here. Carrie responded that although she missed him with all her heart, she would not wish him to be back here because that would mean he would continue to be tormented and in pain. She said that he was with his Jesus, free from the pain and dancing for joy. I have reminded myself of this story whenever I have been tempted to be selfish and want my son back here with me. To me, Carrie's response was a great example of selfless love—to want your loved one to be free of their pain and experiencing the joy of being in the presence of the King, even if it breaks your heart.

I can truthfully tell you that God has healed the wounds inflicted by Christopher's death. The loss will always be felt, but it has not destroyed me. The key was focusing on God and his truths. It is not an easy thing to do because they are so different from our own. We see this in the Bible, where it tells us that the first will be last, the least shall be the greatest, etc.

When I let go of my own will and my own way of seeing, God was able to lead me out of the dark hole and into the light of acceptance and healing.

We were created for his purpose, and not the other way around. Our children and loved ones were also created by him and for him. He is in control, and we are not.

When we grasp these truths, then acceptance comes. When we remember that we are created as eternal beings, then we know that this life is but a breath for each one of us. But all of us go on in spirit forever. I know that I will see Christopher again. And that joy and expectation replaced the pain and the grief.

The Bible tells us to seek and find, to knock and it will be opened. This verse points us to God and to his truth. When we look at things through his eyes and gain his perspective, we are then able to do extraordinary things.

Thank you for sharing my story, and I hope you no longer feel alone in your own journey.

God has a purpose for each one of you. Your pain can be used to help others, and it will give you great joy when that happens. We have been chosen to walk a very scary, dark path, but we have not walked it alone.

Jesus has been with us every step of the way, even when we could not feel him. He cried with us, grieved with us, and carried us when we could no longer move forward on our own.

Find your purpose and a way of honoring your loved one. Tell their story and give them a legacy that is worthy of them. They were warriors lost on the battlefield, and it is up to us to pick up their weapons and keep fighting.

God bless you! I am praying for you, even though I do not know your name. When I lift you up to the Father, I know that he knows who you are.

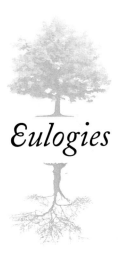

Eulogies

Let no unwholesome word proceed out of your
mouth but only such a word as is good for edi-
fication according to the need of the moment,
so that it will give grace to those who hear.
Ephesians 4:29

I wanted to include Jeanne's and my eulogy so that
you could see where we placed our focus during this
difficult time.

To this day, I can hardly believe that God gave
me the courage and steadfastness to speak at my son's
funeral. But having our focus on using this for his
glory helped us as well.

I have learned that when we see things from God's perspective and keep in mind the eternal consequences of our words and deeds, we gain the strength that is needed to survive the unthinkable.

We know that Christopher's desire was that others come to know Christ as their Savior. That was our desire as well, so all of the plans were made with that in mind.

Jeanne's Eulogy

My name is Jeanne Oweis, and I'm Christopher's aunt. I realize many of you know Christopher as a friend or coworker. But I want to take a few moments to tell you about my Christopher, my soul mate. We may be related by blood as aunt and nephew, but I think we relate to one another more in spirit.

You see, Christopher and I share many of the same passions. I think first of our love for the beauty of God's creation. When Christopher was a young tike, about the age of two, his favorite word was *soutside*. He would constantly run to the door and yell, "Soutside, Mommy, soutside!" And if we weren't careful to keep the door closed and locked, he would be outside and gone in the blink of an eye.

We used to joke amongst ourselves that it would be great for our families to vacation together in Arizona. We agreed—Christopher and I—that we would leave Carrie and Mutaz at the hotel with the kids, and then he and I would hike the Grand Canyon and raft the Colorado! We shared the same mindset. There's not a mountain we couldn't hike or a tree we wouldn't climb.

We both agreed—my Christopher and I— that we could experience God most when we were out in his creation. So when you see the sun paint a mountain at dusk or come across a tree that is begging to be climbed, think of Christopher.

Another passion we share—my Christopher and I—is chocolate! And I don't mean chocolate. I mean *chocolate*! Our personal philosophy on life is this: nothing can be too sweet, and there is no such thing as too much chocolate. Again, we agree, we leave our spouses to each other. Carrie and Mutaz would rather have real food and couldn't care less about dessert. Christopher and I think that is an anathema; we would choose dessert over food any day!

My last visit with Christopher, just two weeks ago, was when he and Carrie came over for my birthday. He came striding in with that Christopher smirk on his face and handed me the most fabulous surprise that he knew only I could appreciate for its value. He brought me a dark chocolate mint cheesecake that he had made himself.

So when you find yourself feasting on a succulent morsel of chocolate or you're tempted to accuse a magnificent dessert of being too sweet, think of Christopher.

The last passion that we share—my Christopher and I—is a passion for people. At times, it may be difficult for people to see the caring, but it's there. You see, Christopher inherited many of the same traits that I inherited, and from the same source, my father and his grandfather, Rex Williams. We learned early in life the power of the expression; we learned *the look*, and we inherited *the smirk*. The *look* comes out if the situation requires, and we can use it to intimidate without saying a word. Try to make us laugh, and you'll get *the smirk*. But most of all, you can't assume we're mad just by the looks on our face.

But that is not all that we inherited from my daddy. You see, Christopher was the only grandchild that got to spend much time with him. And our fondest memories are of Christopher and Daddy out on the pier at the campground with their fishing poles. Daddy loved to fish, and Christopher inherited that love. But that is not the whole story.

You see, my daddy may have loved fishing in the lake, but his real passion was fishing for people. I could not escape this heart passion myself, and I too am compelled to be a *fisher of men*.

For many years, we prayed for Christopher, knowing that the time would come when he would make a decision for Jesus. Christopher wouldn't do anything halfway. It's not his nature. He was determined to be sure he knew what he was doing. When he finally was ready, his commitment was one hundred and ten percent. And when Christopher made the commitment, Christopher caught the heart passion.

Anyone who knows Christopher knows he cared about people. But what you need to understand, and what Christopher was trying to communicate to so many of you, is that you didn't really know him. You see, to really know Christopher in his truest spirit, you have to know his Jesus. Christopher would be the first to tell you that he's human, he has struggles, and he has hardship. But the key is that in spite of all of that, he has Jesus. And regardless of what he struggled with here on earth, his struggles are now over, and he has his Jesus. His struggles are gone, and he has been delivered.

I am compelled to share these thoughts with you and to let you know my Christopher. My Christopher is passionate about nature, passionate about chocolate, passionate about people, but most of all, his passion is that all of you would know his Jesus.

So my challenge to you as you look up at this cross is to think of my Christopher and to know his Jesus.

Deborah's Eulogy

It is important to me that you do not focus on the circumstances of my son's death. We want to celebrate his life, but there is so much more going on here than even that.

We don't want you to focus on the pain of this situation or the struggle that Christopher was having. We want you to know his hope and his purpose and his ultimate desire for each one of you.

Oswald Chambers has said, "Joy means the perfect fulfillment of that which I was created and regenerated, not the successful doing of a thing. The joy our Lord has lay in doing what the Father sent him to do. Think of the satisfaction it will bring when we hear him say, 'Well done, good and faithful servant.'"

Although Christopher was not perfect, he had found redemption and salvation. Out of his love and gratitude to his Jesus, he lived out his faith in many ways. When he saw your need, he met it. When he saw you hurting, he comforted you. When you needed someone there, he was there. He loved unconditionally and selflessly. He did that because he was following the example and commandments of his Lord. He was being, as they say, Jesus with skin on, and he did that in the hope that you would come to know Jesus as he did. His love, loyalty, and generosity were of God. He was the conduit of God's love to you.

That was his heart. That was his purpose. Christopher was a gift to all of us. And we feel blessed to have had the honor to know him here for a short time. But our hope and our joy in the midst of this trial is that we will see him again—this time, for eternity.

Epilogue

It has been six years since Christopher's death, and I wanted you to know how we are doing.

Tom and Corinna graduated from the University of North Carolina-Greensboro in May 2010. They were married in August in a very simple, but beautiful wedding. To honor Christopher, Tom and Joe each wore a pair of his favorite Doc Martin shoes and left an open space in the line of attendants. Tom enlisted in the army and departed for basic training on Christopher's thirty-third birthday (October 26th). They will be moving to Fort Riley Kansas in February 2011.

Joe is still looking for his path in life, but he is a wonderful young man who cares deeply for others.

He is built and looks so much like Christopher that it sometimes it causes us to do a double take. He is carrying Christopher's love of music with him as he seeks his path.

Carrie and Cordie moved to Virginia Beach last summer to be closer to her family. Carrie has decided to go back to graduate school and pursue secondary degrees in counseling. Her heart is leading her to work with military families in dealing with grief and other issues. I think it will be tremendously rewarding for her.

She became a widow at age twenty-five. Christopher was her husband and best friend, and it has not been easy, but she has grown and matured to a wonderful, independent, strong woman with deep convictions. She is a remarkable parent to Cordie.

My darling Cordelia turned six in the summer of 2010. She is my favorite human being in the whole world! We have all been so blessed to have her in our lives. For me, she has been the sun shining through the clouds, a soothing balm over painful wounds.

She lights up my world and keeps me smiling. When she stays with me, we snuggle in bed and I am reminded of the times when I did that with her dad. With her childlike faith and innocent acceptance, she has shown me the way out of this dark tunnel. She always looks up and forward. She takes pleasure out of the simple things in life. Through her example, we relearned the secret to living in this fallen world.

As for me, I am now teaching a small group of women in the same church I have been attending since 1997. We call ourselves the Daughters of Zion, and it is full of women who, like myself, couldn't find a class they fit into. Our focus is on being transparent and affording a safe environment for each one to learn to lean on the others. In November of this year (2010), one of these women lost her thirty-one-year-old son in a car accident and another one lost her husband to cancer. They have told me that in the past year and a half, my story of God's grace through my own loss helped to prepare them for their own. That is the most precious blessing that I could receive.

I have also been promoted to the director at the nonprofit ministry where I have been involved for thirteen years. Following the story of Christopher's abuse, many of my friends and colleagues came out with their own stories. Out of that came *Journey*, a support group for survivors of abuse. It is another example of God taking what Satan meant for evil and turning it into something beautiful. Many people have found the healing that Christopher never did through this group.

I also took up painting a few years ago and find it very therapeutic. I give away a lot of my work as gifts but also sell some of it at local arts and crafts shows.

But the biggest change in me has been that I no longer hesitate through life burdened with fear. I have been through my worst nightmare, and I not only survived, but also, with God's love and grace, I have overcome my own bondages and strongholds.

We are survivors, and we are marching forward through life. I believe that if you look to God in the midst of your pain, you too will find *Joy in the Mourning*!

God's blessings!
Deborah

Resources

Helpful websites:

suicideandmentalhealthassociationinternational.org

Survivorsofsuicide.com

Childsuicide.org

Suicidememorialwall.com

Organizations:

American Foundation for Suicide Prevention (afsp. org)

National Institute of Mental Health (nih.gov)

Yellow Ribbon Suicide Prevention (yellowribbon.org)

Music:

"Beauty Will Rise" by Steven Curtis Chapman

Help for victims of abuse:

Open Hearts Ministry (ohmin.org)

Books:

"Why" by Ann Graham Lotz

Photos

Cordie and Mommy before they head out to first day

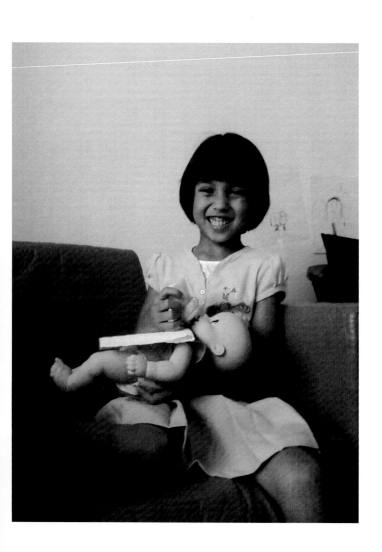